Samuel Perkins

Proceedings at the laying of the corner stone of the new public buildings on Penn square,

In the city of Philadelphia, July 4, 1874;

.

Samuel Perkins

Proceedings at the laying of the corner stone of the new public buildings on Penn square,
In the city of Philadelphia, July 4, 1874;

ISBN/EAN: 9783337713362

Printed in Europe, USA, Canada, Australia, Japan

Cover: Foto ©ninafisch / pixelio.de

More available books at **www.hansebooks.com**

PROCEEDINGS

AT THE

Laying of the Corner Stone

OF THE

NEW PUBLIC BUILDINGS

ON

PENN SQUARE,

IN THE

CITY OF PHILADELPHIA,

JULY 4, 1874;

WITH A DESCRIPTION OF THE BUILDINGS, THE STATISTICS AND PROGRESS
OF THE WORK, AND A SUMMARY OF LEGISLATIVE AND MUNICIPAL
ACTION RELATING TO THE UNDERTAKING; WITH A BRIEF
HISTORY OF EVENTS PERTAINING THERETO.

·

PRINTED FOR THE COMMISSIONERS.

HENRY B. ASHMEAD, PRINTER,

1102 AND 1104 SANSOM STREET, PHILADELPHIA.

COMMISSIONERS

For the Erection of the Public Buildings.

THOMAS J. BARGER,	THOMAS E. GASKILL,
WILLIAM BRICE,	A. WILSON HENSZEY,
LEWIS C. CASSIDY,	JOHN L. HILL,
SAMUEL W. CATTELL,	HIRAM MILLER,
MAHLON H. DICKINSON,	RICHARD PELTZ,
ROBERT W. DOWNING,	SAMUEL C. PERKINS,

WILLIAM S. STOKLEY.

OFFICERS.

President.
SAMUEL C. PERKINS.

Secretary.
FRANCIS DE HAES JANVIER.

Treasurer.
PETER A. B. WIDENER.

Solicitor.
CHARLES H. T. COLLIS.

Architect.
JOHN McARTHUR, Jr.

Superintendent.
WILLIAM C. McPHERSON.

The bill providing for the erection of New Public Buildings for the City of Philadelphia, passed both branches of the State Legislature in April, 1870, and on the 5th of the following August, the Governor affixed his signature thereto.

AN ACT

FOR THE

Erection of the Public Buildings.

-

An Act *to provide for the erection of all the Public Buildings required to accommodate the Courts, and for all Municipal purposes, in the City of Philadelphia, and to require the appropriation by said City, of Penn Squares, at Broad and Market Streets, to the Academy of Fine Arts, the Academy of Natural Sciences, the Franklin Institute, and the Philadelphia Library, in the event of the said Squares not being selected by a vote of the people, as the site for the Public Buildings for said City.*

Section I. BE IT ENACTED by the Senate and House of Representatives of the Commonwealth of Pennsylvania, in General Assembly met, and it is hereby enacted by the authority of the same : That THEODORE CUYLER, JOHN RICE, SAMUEL C. PERKINS, JOHN PRICE WETHERILL, LEWIS C. CASSIDY, HENRY M. PHILLIPS, WILLIAM L. STOKES, WILLIAM DEVINE, the MAYOR OF THE CITY OF PHILADELPHIA, and the PRESIDENTS OF SELECT AND COMMON COUNCILS, for the time being, are constituted Commissioners for the erection of the Public Buildings required to accommodate the Courts, and for all Municipal purposes, in the City of Philadelphia, who shall organize within thirty days, procure such plans for the said buildings adapted to either of said sites hereinafter named, as in their judgment may be needful ; appoint of their own number, a President, and from other than their own number, a Secretary, Treasurer, Solicitor, a competent Architect and assistants, and other employees ; fix the compensation of each person employed by them, and do all other acts necessary in their judgment to carry out the intent of this act in relation to said Public Buildings; fill any vacancies which may happen by death, resignation, or otherwise, and if in the judgment of said Commission, they shall deem it advisable to increase their number, they may, by a vote of a majority of their whole number, increase said Commission from time to time to any number not exceeding thirteen. The said Commissioners are hereby authorized and directed to locate said buildings on either Washington Square or Penn Square, as may be determined by a vote of the legally qualified voters of the City of Philadelphia, at the next general election in October, one thousand eight hundred and seventy, and the Sheriff shall issue his proclamation, and the City Commissioners and other proper officers of said City, shall provide all things that may be needful to enable the voters to decide by ballot, their choice of a site for said Public Buildings, and the Return Clerks shall certify to the Prothonotary, the result of said election in the usual form required for other elections. And as soon as said choice is determined by a vote of the people, as provided in this act, the said Commissioners shall, within thirty days thereafter, advertise for proposals, and make all needful contracts for the construction of said buildings, as soon thereafter as may be found practicable, which contracts shall be valid and binding in law upon the City, and upon the Contractors, when approved by a majority of the said Board of Commissioners; and the said Commissioners shall make requisition on the Councils of said City, prior to the first day of December in each year, for the amount of money required by them for the purposes of the Commission for the succeeding year, and said Councils shall levy a special tax, sufficient to raise the amount so required. *Provided*, That said Councils may at any time make appropriations out of the annual tax in aid of the purposes of this act. *And provided further*, That the amount to be expended by said Commissioners shall be strictly limited to the sum required to satisfy their contracts for the erection of said buildings, and for the proper and complete furnishing thereof; and as soon as any part of said buildings may be completed and furnished ready for occupancy, they shall be occupied by the Courts, or such branch of the Municipal Government as they are intended for by said Commissioners; and upon the completion of a sufficient portion of said buildings to accommodate the Courts and Municipal

Offices, the buildings now occupied by them respectively shall be vacated and removed, and upon the entire completion of the new buildings, all the present buildings on Independence Square, except Independence Hall, shall be removed, and the ground placed in good condition by said Commission as part of their duty under this act, the expense of which shall be paid out of their general fund provided by this act, and thereupon the said Independence Square shall be and remain a public walk and green for ever.

And be it further provided, That in the event of Washington Square being selected by a majority of votes as the location for the said Public Buildings, then and in that event, the Councils of the City of Philadelphia are hereby authorized, empowered and required to set apart for and convey by proper deeds or grants of conveyance, or by proper assurances of the right to occupy said squares, which the Mayor of Philadelphia shall duly sign and execute under the seal of said City, the four squares of ground, known as Penn Squares, located at the intersection of Broad and Market Streets, in the City of Philadelphia, as laid down on the present map of said City, one to each of the following institutions : the Academy of Fine Arts, the Academy of Natural Sciences, the Franklin Institute, and the Philadelphia Library, for the purpose of allowing them to erect thereon, ornamental and suitable buildings for their respective institutions. The location of such buildings and the plans thereof to be approved by the Commissioners appointed under this act, and their successors in office, together with the time of erection, and all other matters appertaining thereto : *Provided, however,* That all expenses connected with said conveyances, plans, and other information requisite for the said Commission to have, shall be paid by the institutions respectively. In the event of the ultimate selection of Penn Squares as the site for said Public Buildings, the said Commission shall have authority and they are hereby empowered to vacate so much of Market and of Broad Streets, as they may deem needful ; *Provided, however,* That the streets passing around said buildings, shall not be of less width than one hundred feet. It shall be the duty of the Mayor, the City Controller, City Commissioners, and City Treasurer, and of all other officers of the City, and also the duty of the Councils of the City of Philadelphia, to do and per-

8

form all such acts in aid and promotion of the intent and purpose of this Act of Assembly, as said Commission may from time to time require. All laws and parts of laws restricting the uses and purposes of said Squares, or any of them, that may be in conflict with the intention and purpose of this act, be and the same are hereby repealed.

B. B. STRANG,
Speaker of the House of Representatives.

CHARLES H. STINSON,
Speaker of the Senate.

Approved the fifth day of August, Anno Domini one thousand eight hundred and seventy.

JOHN W. GEARY.

PROCEEDINGS

Relative to the Laying of the Corner Stone.

The larger portion of the excavations having been completed, and the foundations being in a good state of forwardness, the following Resolution was unanimously adopted at a stated meeting of the Commissioners, held June 2, 1874:

Resolved, That there be a Committee of five appointed (of which the President shall be chairman), for the purpose of preparing a suitable Corner Stone for the New City Hall, and to make the necessary arrangements for laying the same.

COMMITTEE.

SAMUEL C. PERKINS, *Chairman.*

MAHLON H. DICKINSON,

WILLIAM BRICE,

HIRAM MILLER,

THOMAS J. BARGER.

The Committee resolved that the Corner Stone should be laid with Masonic ceremonies, and a request was made of the R. W. Grand Master of Masons of Pennsylvania, which with his reply thereto was as follows:

OFFICE OF THE
COMMISSIONERS FOR THE ERECTION OF THE PUBLIC BUILDINGS,

PHILADELPHIA, *June* 3, 1874.

ALFRED R. POTTER, ESQ.,
R. W. Grand Master of Masons of Penna.

MY DEAR SIR AND R. W. BRO.:

It is with pleasure that on behalf of the Special Committee to whom were entrusted the arrangements for laying the Corner Stone of the New Municipal Buildings at Penn Square, I have by authority and direction of the Commissioners for the Erection of the Public Buildings, earnestly and cordially to request that the Corner Stone may be laid with Masonic ceremonies by yourself, assisted by the Grand Officers of the R. W. Grand Lodge.

The time appointed is July 4, 1874, at high twelve. It will be my duty, no less than my pleasure, to confer with you and afford every facility and accommodation that may be required, in order that the ceremonies may be conducted with the greatest effect.

Very truly and fraternally yours,

SAMUEL C. PERKINS,
President of Commissioners and Chairman of Committee.

OFFICE OF THE
R. W. THE GRAND MASTER OF FREE AND ACCEPTED MASONS OF PENNA., &c.

MASONIC TEMPLE, PHILADELPHIA, *June* 5, 1874.

SAMUEL C. PERKINS, ESQ.,
President of Commissioners, &c., and Chairman of Committee.

MY DEAR SIR AND BRO.:

It will give me very great pleasure to comply with the request of the Commissioners for the Erection of the Public Buildings, contained in your note of the 3d inst., viz., to lay the Corner Stone of the Public Buildings, July 4, 1874, at high twelve.

I shall be pleased to confer with you on the subject, at your earliest convenience, at my office.

Truly and fraternally yours,

ALFRED R. POTTER,
Grand Master.

The Mayor of the City acceded to a request to preside.

OFFICE OF THE

COMMISSIONERS FOR THE ERECTION OF THE PUBLIC BUILDINGS,

PHILADELPHIA, *June* 16, 1874.

Hon. Wm. S. Stokley,

    Mayor of Philadelphia.

Sir :

    The Corner Stone of the New Public Buildings for the City of Philadelphia is to be laid with due ceremony on Saturday, July 4, 1874, at twelve o'clock noon. It is deemed appropriate that the Chief Magistrate of the City should preside on the occasion, and by direction of the Commissioners I have the pleasure to request that you will honor the occasion not only by your presence, but by acting as presiding officer.

        Very respectfully,

                SAMUEL C. PERKINS,

                    President of the Commissioners.

MAYOR'S OFFICE, OF THE CITY OF PHILADELPHIA,

                June 18, 1874.

Samuel C. Perkins, Esq.,

    Dear Sir :

    Your communication of the 16th inst., was received this A. M. It will afford me gratification to comply with your request to preside on the occasion of laying the Corner Stone of the New Public Buildings for the City of Philadelphia, on Saturday, July 4th, next.

        I am, very respectfully,

                W. S. STOKLEY,

                    Mayor.

Invitations to be present were extended to

The President of the United States,

The Governor of the State,

The Heads of Departments of the United States and of the
State,

The Senators and Representatives from Pennsylvania,

The Judges of the Supreme Court of the State,

The Judges of the United States Courts meeting in the City,

The Judges of the Courts of Common Pleas, and of the District Court of the City and County,

The Heads of the City Departments,

The City Councils,

The former Mayors of the City,

Officers of the Army and Navy stationed or residing in the
City,

Foreign Consuls and Vice-Consuls,

Officers of the United States Government in the City,

The Leading Clergy,

Officers and Members of the Centennial Commission,

The Contractors on the Building; and a large number of other
prominent and distinguished citizens.

Upwards of ten thousand tickets were printed and issued to
citizens who applied for them; these tickets secured admission
to the southern portion of the enclosure.

The Hon. Benjamin Harris Brewster, LL. D., having been
invited to deliver an Address, accepted the invitation.

OFFICE OF THE
COMMISSIONERS FOR THE ERECTION OF THE PUBLIC BUILDINGS,

PHILADELPHIA, *June* 3, 1874.

HON. BENJAMIN HARRIS BREWSTER,

MY DEAR SIR:

The Corner Stone of the New Public Buildings for the use of this Municipality in all its branches and departments, is to be laid at noon, July 4, 1874.

And it is with very great pleasure that on behalf of the Committee of Arrangements I have to state, that with entire unanimity you have been selected to deliver an Address appropriate to the occasion; and to request in the name of the Commissioners that you will kindly undertake this duty, which from your well known interest in and thorough identification with every thing pertaining to the welfare of this City, you are so eminently calculated for.

Hoping for an early and favorable response,

I remain very truly and respectfully yours,

SAMUEL C. PERKINS,
President of Commissioners and Chairman of Committee.

706 WALNUT STREET, PHILADELPHIA.

TO SAMUEL C. PERKINS, ESQ.,
President of Commissioners, &c., Chairman of Committee, &c.

MY DEAR SIR:

I have the honor to acknowledge the receipt of your letter of the 3d of June, 1874, and request you to say to the Committee for me that I accept the polite invitation, so courteously conveyed by you, to deliver the Address upon the laying of the Corner Stone of the New Public Buildings, at noon, July 4, 1874.

I am with respect,

Your obedient servant,

BENJAMIN HARRIS BREWSTER.

9th June, 1874.

The northeast angle of the tower was fixed upon as the place where the Corner Stone should be laid. The whole of the area of the foundation for the tower was floored over, except immediately about the location of the stone, thus affording ample room for the effective performance of the Masonic Ceremonies. On the north, east and west sides of this area, an amphitheatre was erected with benches rising from the floor, for the accommodation of the spectators. The whole was decorated with flags and bunting, and protected by a large awning.

The Corner Stone itself was of a block of fine white marble weighing about eight tons, from the Lee quarries, which were to furnish the material for the superstructure above the basement. Upon the upper side a cavity was made for the reception of a copper box in which the coins, documents, &c., were to be deposited. It was arranged that one face of the stone should be exposed to view from the interior space in the centre of the tower foundation, and upon this face was cut the following inscription :

CORNER STONE

OF THE

PUBLIC BUILDINGS OF THE CITY OF PHILADELPHIA,

LAID JULY 4, 1874,

In the presence of the Mayor of the City, the Select and Common Councils, Heads of Departments, and other distinguished Civil, Military and Naval Officials, and a large concourse of Citizens,

By ALFRED R. POTTER, Esq.,

R. W. GRAND MASTER OF MASONS OF PENNSYLVANIA AND MASONIC JURISDICTION THEREUNTO BELONGING, ASSISTED BY HIS GRAND OFFICERS, AND ACCORDING TO THE ANCIENT CEREMONIES OF THE CRAFT.

Orator—BENJAMIN HARRIS BREWSTER.

President of the United States—ULYSSES S. GRANT.   Governor of Pennsylvania—JOHN F. HARTRANFT.   Mayor of Philadelphia—WILLIAM S. STOKLEY.

ARCHITECT—JOHN McARTHUR, Jr.   **Commissioners for the Erection of the Public Buildings.**   SUPERINTENDENT—WILLIAM C. McPHERSON.

Act of Assembly, August 5, 1870.

PRESIDENT—SAMUEL C. PERKINS.

THOS. J. BARGER,	SAMUEL W. CATTELL,	MAHLON H. DICKINSON,	THOMAS E. GASKILL,	JOHN L. HILL,	RICHARD PELTZ,
WILLIAM BRICE,	LEWIS C. CASSIDY,	ROBT. W. DOWNING,	A. WILSON HENSZEY,	HIRAM MILLER,	WM. S. STOKLEY.
SECRETARY—FRANCIS DE HAES JANVIER.		TREASURER—PETER A. B. WIDENER.		SOLICITOR—CHARLES H. T. COLLIS.	

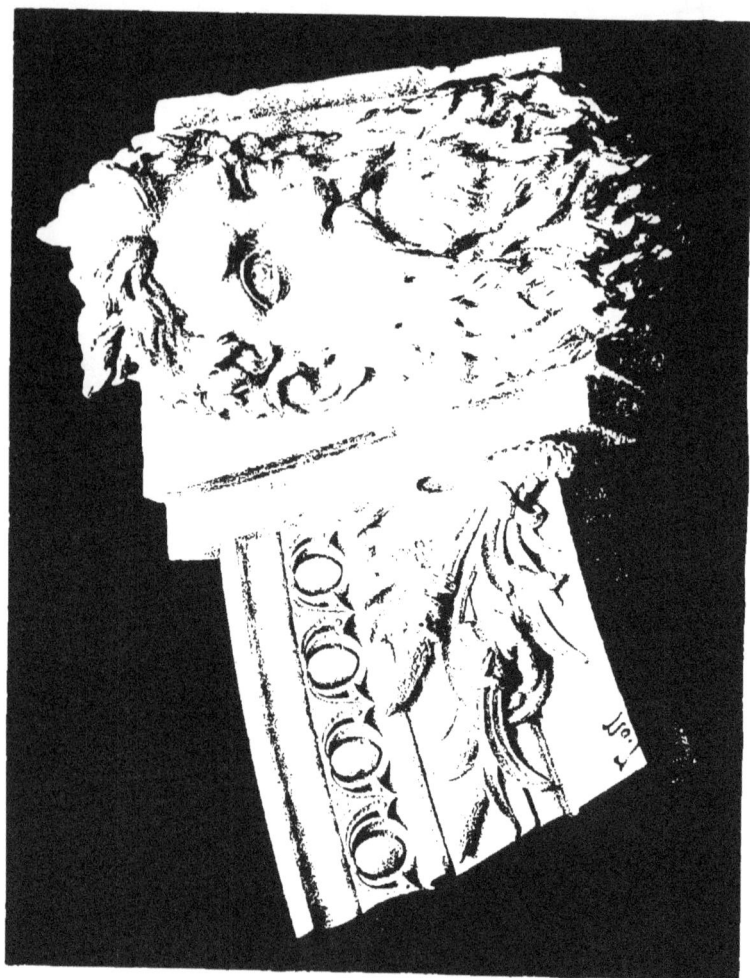

CEREMONIES

OF THE

𝕷𝖆𝖞𝖎𝖓𝖌 𝖔𝖋 𝖙𝖍𝖊 𝕮𝖔𝖗𝖓𝖊𝖗 𝕾𝖙𝖔𝖓𝖊.

PRESIDENT OF THE DAY,

THE HON. WILLIAM S. STOKLEY,

MAYOR OF THE CITY.

2

Officers of the R. W. Grand Lodge of Pennsylvania

WHO OFFICIATED IN THE CEREMONIES OF THE OCCASION.

ALFRED R. POTTER,   R. W. GRAND MASTER.
ROBERT CLARK, .   R. W. DEPUTY GRAND MASTER.
J. MADISON PORTER,   R. W. SENIOR GRAND WARDEN.
MICHAEL NISBET, .   R. W. JUNIOR GRAND WARDEN.
THOMAS R. PATTON,   R. W. GRAND TREASURER.
JOHN THOMSON,   R. W. GRAND SECRETARY.

Grand Chaplains.

REV. WM. SUDDARDS, D.D.,   REV. J. W. CUSTIS,
REV. ROBERT H. PATTISON, D.D.,   REV. EDGAR M. LEVY.

Senior Grand Deacon.

ISAAC VANDUSEN, Lodge No. 441, Philadelphia.

Junior Grand Deacon.

WILLIAM J. KELLY, Lodge No. 59, Philadelphia.

Grand Stewards.

GEORGE B COLE, Lodge No. 315, Shippensburg.
JAMES MORRELL, Lodge No. 114, Philadelphia.

Grand Marshal.

GEORGE W. WOOD, Lodge No. 67, Philadelphia.

Grand Sword Bearer.

A. J. KAUFFMAN, Lodge No. 286, Columbia

Grand Pursuivant.

S. KINGSTON McKAY, Lodge No. 72. Philadelphia.

Grand Tyler.

HARRISON G. CLARK, Lodge No. 158, Philadelphia.

R. W. Bros. PETER FRITZ, P. G. M.; SAMUEL C. PERKINS, P. G. M., and also R. W. P. G. J. W. and Grand Representative of the M. W. Grand Lodge of Louisiana, and Grand Representative of M. W. Grand Lodge of Canada; and R. W Bro. MARSHALL B. SMITH, R. W. S. G. W. of the M. W. Grand Lodge of New Jersey, were present.

The following brethren, by special appointment of the Grand Marshal, acted as his Assistants :

HENRY J. WHITE,   THOMAS BROWN,
CHAS. H. KINGSTON,   WILLIAM T. REYNOLDS.

The Music was furnished by
McClurg's Liberty Cornet Band of Philadelphia.

Benjamin K. McClurg, *Leader.*

Ceremonies.

" The Commissioners for the Erection of the Public Buildings," with "the Right Worshipful Grand Lodge of Free and Accepted Masons of Pennsylvania, and Masonic Jurisdiction thereunto belonging," assembled at the Masonic Temple, at 11 o'clock, A. M., and marched in procession to the site of the new Public Buildings, entering the enclosure by the west gate.

When the procession reached the west end of the platform prepared for the Grand Lodge, it halted, opened to the right and left, and the R. W. Grand Master, preceded by the Grand Sword Bearer, and followed by the Grand Lodge Officers, the Commissioners, and the members of the Grand Lodge, advanced through the opened ranks to the east of the platform.

As the procession entered and advanced the band played "The Belphegor March."—*Brepsant.*

The R. W. Grand Master directed the Grand Officers to take their appropriate stations and places.

Hon. William S. Stokley, Mayor of the City and *ex officio* one of the Commissioners, took his seat as Presiding Officer of the day, on the north side of the platform, having on his right, Samuel C. Perkins, Esq., President of the Commissioners, and on his left, Hon. Benjamin Harris Brewster, LL.D., the Orator chosen for the occasion.

The Grand Marshal proclaimed—SILENCE! SILENCE! SILENCE!

The R. W. Deputy Grand Master addressed the R. W. Grand Master:

Right Worshipful Sir: " The Commissioners for the Erection of the Public Buildings," for the City of Philadelphia, have requested you to perform the ceremony of laying the Corner Stone. The necessary arrangements have been made by the Commissioners, and I have now the pleasure to present to you their President.

The President of the Commissioners addressed the R. W. Grand Master:

Right Worshipful Sir: The Committee charged with the duty of preparing the Corner Stone have completed their labors, and it is now ready to be laid.

The R. W. Grand Master replied:

Mr. President: Thanking the Commissioners for the honor paid to the craft, in the invitation to the R. W. Grand Lodge of Pennsylvania to lay the Corner Stone of the New Public Buildings of this City, we shall now proceed to perform that duty, according to our ancient usages and customs.

INVOCATION.—By Bro. the Rev. J. W. Custis, Grand Chaplain.

O, Thou Sovereign Architect of the Universe, in Thy name we assemble upon this day which Thou hast sanctified as commemorative of national liberty! We lift our hands and our hearts unto Thee, O Creator and Father. Deign to look upon us from the throne of Thy majesty, even upon us, the unworthy supplicants of Thy favor. Thou hast taught us to look unto Thee in all the undertakings of life; to count upon Thy help in every laudable enterprise. Bow the heavens and come down, O Thou glorious Being. We invoke Thy presence. We invoke Thy blessing upon the work of our hands to-day.

Almighty God, we thank Thee for this day, its hallowed associations, precious memories, and auspicious tokens for the future of our land. For the stability of our National Government, and of the government of this Commonwealth, we thank Thee. Thou hast given unto us great deliverance, inasmuch as the nation, but a little while since storm-tossed as a bark upon an angry sea, whose bloody waves mounted to the very heavens, has been rescued by Thy hand, and brought into a tranquil harbor.

We beseech Thee, our God, let Thy blessing continue upon our Nation, Commonwealth, and City. Bless the President of the United States, the legislative and judicial officers of the land, the Governor of this great State, and all who are united with him in authority; the Mayor, Councils, and all the chosen servants of the people of this City. May they all be men of God, in whom Thou canst find delight, and by whom Thou wilt bring upon the people great prosperity.

And now, O great Architect of the Universe, remember Thy servants who have been called to the performance of solemn duties in the consecration of this edifice. Lend Thine aid and bestow Thy benediction as Thy servant shall prepare and lay the Corner Stone, for "Except the Lord build the house, they labor in vain that build it." May the structure knit together by this stone, in the beauty and grandeur of its material parts, typify the abiding presence of that righteousness which alone exalteth a nation. Direct by Divine wisdom the commission, the architect, and the builders. And when the building, completed, appears even from afar like a mount of alabaster topped with golden spires, may it be to the city as a watch tower and as a strong defence. Anoint with heavenly wisdom the men who shall preside within its walls, so that what they do may be so manifestly right that they may be unto the people as the oracles of God.

O, Thou Sovereign Architect of the Universe, have respect unto the prayer of Thy servant, and to his supplication, to hearken unto the cry and to the prayer of Thy servant and Thy people. That Thine eyes may be open night and day toward the place consecrated in Thy name.

We beseech Thee, for the sake of the Anointed One, who reignest in indescribable glory for ever and ever. Amen.

Response by the Brethren.

Amen. So mote it be. Amen.

The R. W. Grand Master directed the R. W. Grand Treasurer to place the documents, coins, and other valuable articles in the Corner Stone.

The R. W. Grand Treasurer having deposited the articles in a copper, glass-lined box, the lid was securely fastened and the box placed in the cavity in the Corner Stone, which was filled in with cement and covered with a black marble slab, on which were inscribed the names of the Commissioners, and of the Architect and Superintendent.

The R. W. Grand Treasurer addressed the R. W. Grand Master :

Right Worshipful Sir: The coins and other valuable presents, set apart to be placed in the Corner Stone of the New Public Buildings, are now duly deposited there ; and your directions have been faithfully obeyed.

The R. W. Grand Master directed the R. W. Grand Secretary to read a list of the articles so deposited, as follows:

List of Articles Deposited in the Corner Stone.[*]

Constitution of the United States.

Constitution of Pennsylvania.

Charter of the City of Philadelphia.

Elevation and Plans of New Public Buildings.

Act of Assembly establishing the Board of Commissioners, with list of Commissioners and their Officers.

Programme of Ceremonies of Laying the Corner Stone. Proceedings of the R. W. Grand Lodge of F. & A. M. of Pennsylvania, for 1873, and names of Grand Officers officiating in laying the Corner Stone.

List of Officers of the R. W. G. L. of F. & A. M. of Penna.

Manual of Councils, 1874, containing Lists of the Members, and also of all Officers connected with the Government of the City and its several Departments and Public Institutions, and of the County Officers.

Annual Message of the Mayor, 1874.

Annual Reports of the several Departments of the City Government, 1874.

Annual Reports of various Public Institutions of Philadelphia, 1874.

Copies of all the Daily Papers of Philadelphia, July 4, 1874.

---

[*] For particular details see post p. 57.

Copies of the latest numbers of Weekly Papers published in Philadelphia.

Copies of sundry Monthly Publications issued in Philadelphia.

Proof set of all the Coins of the United States, for the year 1874.

MEDALS—

    Washington—Presidency Relinquished.

    Army—Major-Genl. Jackson—Capture of New Orleans.

    Navy—Capt. Bainbridge—Capture of the Java.

    Sub-National—Penna. Volunteers—Action on Lake Erie.

    Miscellaneous—"Let us have Peace."

                Emancipation Proclamation.

                Lincoln and Grant.

                Grant's Indian Peace Medal.

INSTRUMENTAL MUSIC.—Cadet Galop—*McClurg.*

The R. W. Grand Master then addressed the R. W. Deputy Grand Master:

R. W. Deputy Grand Master: It is my will and pleasure that the Corner Stone of the New Public Buildings be now laid. You will announce the same to the R. W. Senior Grand Warden, that he may announce it to the R. W. Junior Grand Warden, with directions then to proclaim the same to the Brethren, that all present may govern themselves accordingly.

The R. W. Deputy Grand Master addressed the R. W. Senior Grand Warden:

It is the R. W. Grand Master's will and pleasure that the Corner Stone of the New Public Buildings be now laid. You will announce the same to the R. W. Junior Grand Warden, with directions then to proclaim the same to the Brethren, that all present may govern themselves accordingly.

The R. W. Senior Grand Warden addressed the R. W. Junior Grand Warden:

It is the R. W. Grand Master's will and pleasure that the Corner Stone of the New Public Buildings be now laid. You will proclaim the same to the Brethren, that all present may govern themselves accordingly.

The R. W. Junior Grand Warden proclaimed:

Brethren: Take notice, it is the R. W. Grand Master's will and pleasure, that the Corner Stone of the New Public Buildings be now laid. You will therefore govern yourselves accordingly.

The R. W. Grand Master addressed the R. W. Deputy Grand Master:

Right Worshipful Sir and Brother: You will see that the Craftsmen have well and truly prepared the Corner Stone to be laid.

The R. W. Deputy Grand Master addressed the R. W. Junior Grand Warden:

You will now see that the Craftsmen have prepared the Stone, and that it is True and Trusty. Test it with the Plumb, and report to me if you are satisfied with the work of the Craftsmen.

The R. W. Junior Grand Warden left his station with the Plumb, and proceeded to the Stone, tested it and said:

R. W. Deputy Grand Master: I find the Stone plumb, and that the Craftsmen have prepared the Corner Stone, True and Trusty.

The R. W. Deputy Grand Master addressed the R. W. Senior Grand Warden:

You will now examine and satisfy yourself if the Craftsmen have worked well. Try the Stone with the Level, and report to me the result of your examination.

The R. W. Senior Grand Warden then left his station with the Level, and proceeded to the Stone, tried it and said:

R. W. Deputy Grand Master: I find this Corner Stone Level, and that the Craftsmen have worked well.

The R. W. Deputy Grand Master then proceeded to the Stone with the Square, tested and tried it, returned to his station and addressed the R. W. Grand Master:

R. W. Grand Master: I find the Corner Stone of the New Public Buildings Tried, True, Trusty, Plumb, Level, and Square, and that the Grand Officers have approved the work, and have found it well and duly prepared, and that the Craftsmen have worked well.

The R. W. Grand Master then addressed the R. W. Deputy Grand Master, R. W. Senior Grand Warden, and R. W. Junior Grand Warden :

Right Worshipful Brothers : You will proceed to the Stone, while the laborers and bearers are placing it in its proper position, at the northeast angle of the tower of the building ; you will test and try it with the Plumb, Level, and Square, and report to us if it is well and duly prepared.

The Stone placed in its bed, was then tested and tried by the Grand Officers, who returned to their stations, and the R. W. Deputy Grand Master said :

R. W. Grand Master: The Corner Stone is duly placed, and is now ready to be laid.

INSTRUMENTAL MUSIC.—Corner Stone March—*McClurg*.

The Senior and Junior Grand Deacons then proceeded to the Stone with the Trowel and the Gavel.

The R. W. Grand Master, preceded by the Grand Marshal and Grand Sword Bearer, then proceeded to the Stone, took the Trowel from the Junior Grand Deacon, and having spread cement, the covering stone was lowered into its place by the workmen. The R. W. Grand Master then took the Gavel from the Senior Grand Deacon, and striking the Corner Stone three times therewith returned to his station and announced :

We, ALFRED R. POTTER, Grand Master of Masons of Pennsylvania and Masonic Jurisdiction thereunto belonging, declare this Corner Stone to be Plumb, Level, and Square, and so duly laid according to the Ancient Usages, Customs, and Landmarks of Free Masonry, and may the Great Architect of Heaven and Earth bless the work here begun, and make it memorable to the latest generations.

28

INSTRUMENTAL MUSIC.—Defile Galop—*Arban.*

The Grand Stewards then proceeded to the Stone, bearing the vessels of Corn, Wine, and Oil. The R. W. Deputy Grand Master, with R. W. Grand Wardens, then proceeded to the Stone, and the Grand Steward, presenting to the R. W. Deputy Grand Master the Cornucopia, he dropped the Corn on the Stone and said:

May plenty be showered down on the people of this ancient Commonwealth, and may the labors of the Craft be refreshed by the Great Giver of every good and perfect gift.

The Grand Steward presented the Wine to the R. W. Senior Grand Warden, who poured it on the Stone, and said:

May the health of the Craftsmen employed in erecting the New Public Buildings be preserved to them, and may the Supreme Architect bless and prosper their labors.

The Grand Steward presented the Oil to the R. W. Junior Grand Warden, who dropped it on the Stone, and said:

May the Supreme Ruler of the World vouchsafe unity, peace and prosperity to the people of Pennsylvania, and to the nations of the earth; watch over the interests of the City of Philadelphia and the progress of the New Public Buildings; preserve and protect the Fraternity of Free Masons; make the virtues of the Craft a lesson to the world, and the labors of the Craftsmen easy, and their burdens light.

The Grand Officers then returned to their places.

INSTRUMENTAL MUSIC.—The Beautiful Blue Danube—*Heinecke.*

The President of the Commissioners then presented the Architect to the R. W. Grand Master, saying:

Right Worshipful Sir: Let me present to you JOHN McARTHUR, JR., Esq., the Architect of the New Public Buildings. He has his Craftsmen ready for the work, and desires you to give him the designs from the tressel-board, and the tools of the workmen.

The R. W. Grand Master then handed him plans and tools, and intrusted him with the work.

INSTRUMENTAL MUSIC. — World's Peace Jubilee, Pot-pourri—*Beyer*.

The Grand Marshal then proclaimed—SILENCE! SILENCE! SILENCE!

Brethren: Take notice, that the R. W. Grand Master, Brother ALFRED R. POTTER, Grand Master of Masons of Pennsylvania, and Masonic Jurisdiction thereunto belonging, has this day, at this place, laid the Corner Stone of the New Public Buildings of the City of Philadelphia.

WISDOM! STRENGTH!! FRATERNITY!!!

The Declaration of Independence was then recited by WILLIAM H. MAURICE, ESQ.

INSTRUMENTAL MUSIC.—The Star Spangled Banner.

The HON. WILLIAM S. STOKLEY, Mayor of the City, then introduced the HON. BENJAMIN HARRIS BREWSTER as the Orator of the occasion, who spoke as follows:

MR. PRESIDENT AND GENTLEMEN: These solemn ceremonies having been performed, it is now my duty to say some few words, explaining the history and purpose of this great public work. One hundred and eighty years ago, when this city and this province were a wilderness, William Penn, then the proprietor, dedicated this very spot of ground as the suitable site for the public buildings of his projected city. That such was his act, and such his purpose, has been judicially established as a legal and historic fact; and now we perform the conditions of the grant, and honestly apply the gift to the object of the trust, obeying the intentions of our provident benefactor.

For many years this city has been unprovided with buildings suitable for the convenient performance of the usual and necessary public business.

Before the consolidation of the city, as created by Penn, we were surrounded with outlying incorporated municipalities. Then the business of each and all was transacted with reasonable convenience in the old municipal buildings, and in the halls that had been erected in the districts and townships of the county, but even then the accommodations were wanting for the growing necessities of our courts. Year after year the officers of the county (then a separate and distinct corporation with its own organization and officials), were driven to adopt expedients to supply the courts with convenient apartments. At one time the Supreme Court was held in the Hall of Independence, at another time the Supreme Court, Nisi Prius, was placed in the chapter room of the old, abandoned Masonic Hall, Chestnut Street, above Seventh. During those days the necessities for such buildings for general public uses were few. Since then new and great departments have grown out of what were subordinate clerkships of public employment.

Day by day the want of proper apartments pressed upon the courts and interfered with the administration of justice. Day by day the same want crowded the officials of the city and the people who had business with them. There was hardly a county of any importance in the State that had not buildings larger in proportion to their wants, by a hundred fold, than our crowded and narrow rooms. Different plans had been projected and suggested for supplying this want. From many causes they all failed. Sometimes the fear of the cost hindered the prosecution of the purpose. Then the selection of the locality was in the way, and then the choice of the means by which it was to be done. At last the Legislature of the Commonwealth finally resolved, and by an Act, approved 5th of August, 1870, provided "for the erection of all of the public buildings required to accommodate the courts, and for all municipal purposes in the city of Philadelphia." That Act created the Commission now in charge of this duty, and gave the people of the city the privilege of indicating, by popular vote, whether the buildings should be at Washington Square or at Penn Square, where we now are, and where we have this day witnessed the laying of the corner stone of one of the most majestic and useful structures that adorn, or have adorned, any city of the world. MAY IT LAST FOR EVER!

After the passage of this Act a heated and almost angry opposition was excited; a series of litigations ensued; applications were made to the Legislature; resistance was attempted in the City Councils, and the elements of the most vehement partisan prejudices were used to frustrate the

law or secure its repeal. Then some of us regretted this opposition.
Some thought it too personal, too violent. But since it has passed away
all are reconciled, and believe that it was for the best. Such an event,
conflicting as it did with so many convictions and interests, must excite
opposition, and those who resisted had a right to be heard, and fully heard,
before all of the tribunals, popular, legislative, and judicial. These con-
tentions delayed the action of the commission for any practical result for
full a year. After that, all those obstructions being removed, it proceeded
to act as the law commanded, as the people had directed, and as the courts
had adjudged. What we now do is the product of that action. On the
7th of January, 1871, the work was first begun, by the removal of the
iron railings which enclosed the four squares or plots of ground, into
which the city had converted the whole, in the year 1828, for the purpose of running Market and Broad Streets through the original plot.
Before that the place had been left as it was originally set apart—one
entire square—and in that state had been occupied, at different times,
and in different parts of it, by a Friends' meeting-house, and by the first
water-works established and used for conveying Schuylkill water to the
old city. I remember the small, neat building that graced the centre.
I think it was designed by Latrobe, the famous architect, who adorned
our city with some of its most beautiful structures, and who left the
Capitol buildings at Washington as the highest achievement of his
genius. The very columns that embellished its front now support the
pediment of the Unitarian Church, at the corner of Tenth and Locust
Streets. The bisection of this plot, by these highways, was for the
purpose of temporary public convenience, and to accommodate the railways that were then for the first time introduced, and whose direct
access to the city proper was considered to be of great importance to its
trade and languishing commerce. With the growth of population and
the changes of events that has passed away, indeed the necessity now is
to remove the railways from the thickly-peopled parts, where they are a
dangerous obstruction to trade and the ordinary pursuits of the thousands
who throng their crowded ways. It was at most but a temporary occu-
pation and license, revocable at will, if it were not an unauthorized and
illegal intrusion.

On the 10th of August, 1871, the ground was broken by John Rice,
Esq., then President of the Board of Commissioners, and the first stone
of the foundation was laid at 2 o'clock, P. M., on the 12th day of August,
A. D. 1872. The closing of the streets and placing the building in the
centre of the plot was the subject of much discussion in the Commission
itself. By some it was wished that the streets should remain open, and the

four plots should each contain a structure ; but the final resolution of the Commission was, and is, to place it and keep it where it was intended by Penn that it should be put—in the centre of the whole ten acres. And with this conclusion, I believe, most men now concur. It is the only place where a building of suitable dignity can stand to display its parts in all the beauty of their architectural effect. It will adorn, and not blemish, the highways at whose intersection it is placed, and it will give an air of majesty and grandeur to these long and broad avenues. It is not put in a corner, hidden from view, but it stands out in bold and high relief, commanding admiration. It is placed, as other and similar great structures are, as the centre of human concourse from which all things radiate and to which all things converge. It is surrounded by a grand avenue 135 feet wide, on the southern and eastern and western fronts, and 205 feet wide on the northern front. Neither the view nor way is hindered by it. The view is improved, the effect being magnified—and the way is widened into open spaces of unusual dimensions, but of proportions that harmonize with the magnitude of the building, and answer the convenience of the multitude that will be drawn here to transact public and private affairs. Had the buildings been divided and placed on the four squares, the cost would have been increased and their beauty lost, while the inconvenience to the public would have been great, and the expense of maintaining them with light and heat and water, and the other necessaries, would have been largely multiplied. The highways would have been smaller and narrower and less convenient. In this, as in all that has been done, these Commissioners have wisely followed, not forced, the general public judgment. Mr. John McArthur, Jr., of this city, who had before this been engaged in preparing all the previous plans, which had been the subject of public consideration for many years, was chosen the architect, and his plan adopted. That has been submitted to the public, and it, too, has been justly applauded and approved. I shall not here undertake to describe it by a multitude of words, which can only degenerate into mere rhetorical expletives, and would therefore be unsuitable as well as vulgar. This much, however, I must speak. It is suited for its purpose, it is of sufficient size to answer future wants. It is admirable in its ornaments, while the whole effect is one of massive dignity, worthy of us and our posterity.

I will here give the dimensions, and a few of the details of this remarkable structure. It is 470 feet from east to west, and 486½ feet from north to south, covering an area, exclusive of the court-yard, of nearly four and a half acres. It is probably larger than any single building on this continent. The superstructure consists of a basement story, 18 feet in height, a principal story, of 36 feet, and an upper story, of 31 feet, surmounted by another of 15 feet. The small rooms opening upon the court-yard are each sub-divided in height into two stories, for the purpose of making useful all the space. The several stories will be approached by four large elevators, placed at the intersections of the leading corridors, to make easy the intercourse of citizens with courts, public offices, and departments of city government. In addition to these means of access there will be a grand staircase in each of the four corners of the building, and one in each of the centre pavilions on the north, south, west and east fronts. The entire structure will contain five hundred and twenty rooms, of suitable dimensions, and fitted with every possible convenience, including heat, light, and ventilation, and the whole is to be absolutely fire-proof and indestructible. All of the departments now existing will be abundantly supplied, and a vast amount of surplus room will be left for judicial and other city archives, as well as afford room for all of our growing wants. This is as it ought to be. We provide for the present urgent wants, and protect the people hereafter from those inconveniences under which we now suffer, and which expose our records to ruin and decay, while they seriously obstruct and hurt all branches of business and public duty. It is computed that the entire cost of this work will be near ten millions of dollars, and that it will be completed in ten years from the day when the first spadeful of earth was removed.

To judge of its massive size, I will give you an account of what materials have been consumed in constructing the foundation and the parts of the superstructure you now see before you: 74,000 cubic feet of cement concrete, 636,400 cubic feet of foundation stone, 8,000,000 bricks, 70,000 cubic feet of dressed granite, and 366 tons of iron, including floor beams.

The excavation for the cellars and foundations required the removal of 141,500 cubic yards of earth. A large quantity of the marble for the superstructure has been prepared, and the corner stone is the first block that has yet been set in the building. Here I will end my details. To be more minute would be tedious and prolix; but this much should be given to properly advise the public.

Let me state with accuracy to what purposes the building will be devoted, and who will occupy it the day it is ready for public use, that you may see and know what are our wants.

The Mayor will require for the use of his office and of the police at least twelve commodious rooms.

34

The City Council Chambers and their officers will need . 15
The City Treasurer, ... 3
The City Controller, ... 5
Law Department, ... 9
Water Department, ... 7
Highways, Bridges and Sewers, ... 4
Survey Department, ... 4
Markets and City Property, ... 2
Building Inspectors, ... 2
Boiler Inspectors, ... 2
Health Office, ... 6
Fire Department, ... 4
Receiver of Taxes, ... 5
Police and Fire-alarm Telegraph, . . . 2
Guardians of the Poor, ... 3
Port Wardens, ... 2
City Commissioners, ... 6
Coroner, ... 4
Girard Estates, ... 2
Board of Education, ... 6
Gas Office, ... 1
Park Commissioners, ... 1
Board of Revision, ... 4
Collector of Delinquent Taxes, ... 3
Courts, 13 rooms, with accommodations for the Prothonotaries
and Clerks, for the Law Library, witness and jury rooms, and
District Attorney.
Recorder of Deeds, 4
Register of Wills, 4
Sheriff, . . 4

At this time the city rents apartments for the Recorder of Deeds, in the Philadelphia National Bank ; for the City Controller and Treasurer, in the Girard Bank ; the Law Buildings on Fifth Street, for the Law Department ; of the American Philosophical Society, for the Water Department ; and for the Survey Department, in No. 224 South Fifth Street ; in No. 723 Arch Street, for the Tax Office and Board of Revision ; and the southwest corner of Fifth and Walnut Streets for the Department of Markets and City Property ; and for these insecure and unsuited places it pays a rent of $41,300. These I mention that it may be known and seen how scattered, costly and unfit are our present accommodations for public purposes.

It will now be proper for me to speak a few words of the extent of our City of Homes, as it has been called,—of its large accommodations for its people,—of its great public improvements for public necessities and private comfort. This I will do in a cursory way, as the occasion and the time will not admit of precision and detail ; but it should be done, to show how fit this structure in all its magnitude of dimensions is for the community it is intended to supply, and how it harmonizes in all things with that which we have around us and about us in daily use, and how essential it is to construct it as it is designed, if we are to have a provident regard for the manifest wants of the future. I have seen and lived in almost all of the capitals of Europe, and I have read of all of the great cities of the world ; but I have never seen or read of such a city as this is. There is no town in the world, of its dimensions or population, and there never has been one, that possesses such accommodations for its people.

Artisans, and even laborers live with us as they never lived before. Men whose daily earnings in other cities will hardly sustain life and provide a shelter for themselves and their families, except in the most rude, coarse, scanty and crowded way, are here the occupants of single and comfortable dwellings, and thousands of them the owners of their own houses.

The effect of this upon the mental and moral condition of the citizens is evident, even to transient visitors. We have no such class here as the poor workingman ; our city is filled with workmen, independent, prosperous freemen, who bring up families of boys with habits of thrift and industry, to go out into life prepared and resolved to earn homes, because they have enjoyed them in their happy childhood, and with good girls, who are certain of provision for life with a comfortable house for their families, because they are trained to keep those homes with tidiness and economy, and because they are raised with a race of men who honor and love their families, and find their only sense of content in the cultivation of the domestic affections. This is true, every word of it true, of Philadelphia and its workmen. At the beginning of the year 1873, we had 134,740 buildings of all kinds. Of these 124,302 were dwelling houses, occupied by families. They exceed the following cities by the following numbers :

New York, by over	60,000
Brooklyn, by over	78,000
St. Louis, by over	84,000
Baltimore, by over	83,000
Chicago, by over	79,000
Boston, by over .	94,000
Cincinnati, by over	99,000

This city has a population of near 800,000, and they live in an area of 129½ square miles. It has 1000 miles of streets and roads opened for use, and over 500 miles of these are paved. It is lighted by near ten thousand gas lamps. The earth beneath conceals and is penetrated by 134 miles of sewers, over 600 miles of gas mains and 546 miles of water pipes. We have over 212 miles of city railways, and near 1794 city railroad cars passing over these railroads daily, 3025 steam boilers, over 400 public schools, with suitable buildings, and over 1600 school teachers, and over 80,000 pupils. We have over 34,000 bath-rooms, most of which are supplied with hot water, and for the use of the water, at low rates, our citizens pay more than a million of dollars annually. We have over 400 places of public worship, and accommodations in them for 300,000 persons.

We have near 9000 manufactories, having a capital of $185,000,000, employing 145,000 hands, the annual product of whose labor is over $384,000,000. We exported in 1873, in value, over $34,000,000, and we imported in value over $26,000,000. The amount paid for duties in gold was near eight millions and a half. The real estate, as assessed for taxation, was over $518,000,000, and we collected near $9,000,000 for taxes. Our funded debt, including the gas loan, in January, 1873, was $51,697,147 67, and our annual outlay in 1873, inclusive of interest on our debt, was $-,726,123. We have parks and public squares, and Fairmount Park, which is one of them, contains 2991 acres, and is one of the largest parks in the world, and was enjoyed in 1873 by near 3,000,000 of people.

From this we can understand for whom we are now building, and why the outlay proposed is provident and necessary. We can also see in a partial way where our money has gone, but we can see with sufficient fulness how providently and judiciously most of it has been expended, when we behold this list of stupendous improvements, millions of which lie beneath the surface of the earth, and millions of which we drive over and walk over, unheeding the cost of the conveniences and comforts we are daily using in the paved, curbed, watered, drained and lighted highways, on which front, for over 2000 miles, 124,302 neat and comfortable homes. I said, we can see in a partial way where our money has gone, because near twelve millions of the debt was incurred for the expenses of the civil war. But even that we can see and value, when, as the fruit of it, we can behold around us not only our own comfortable and peaceful homes, but we feel by its outlay, made with generous prodigality in such a cause, that we have saved a country and a free home for ourselves and for others in this land, and in foreign lands; and we feel that we have also shown, that a republic can "maintain a perfect union, establish justice, insure domestic tranquillity, provide for the common defence, promote the general welfare, and secure the blessings of liberty for themselves and their posterity."

Of all the cities in this nation, Philadelphia is pre-eminently American. Philadelphia's characteristics and customs, the habits and peculiarities of the people, are essentially American. The vast body of its population is chiefly the product of its own people, who were here almost from the beginning. The descendants of the men who were here at its foundation, and were here at the outbreak of the Revolution, are the men who now compose the body of its citizens, who do its work, carry on its trades, make its ordinances, control its offices, own its property, and fill the stations of public usefulness and dignity. We are not governed by strangers, and have never been willing to submit to such rule. We have a manly local pride of citizenship; other seaboard cities are provincial, or filled with strangers from other parts of the nation and from other countries; and the Western cities are, like New York, the homes of new men from old places.

If a foreigner were to ask me, where will I find a real American, untouched in his character and nationality by the ever-drifting tide of emigration, domestic and foreign, and with no taint of provincial narrowness, I would say, go to Philadelphia, and there you will find just such men and women by the hundreds of thousands. There you will find a provident, steadfast race, the sons for over six generations of provident, steadfast ancestors; real Americans, bone of their bone, flesh of their flesh. Early in our career we commanded the foreign and domestic commerce of the colonies, and till 1820 this city was the commercial metropolis of the country. For a time that ascendancy passed away, and New York, by her internal improvements, acquired the trade we had lost. While we thus ruled, we ruled grandly, and we have never forgotten our dignity. The sentiment that then prevailed with our people still prevails. Then they embellished our city with works of architecture, equalled nowhere in the Union in beauty and fitness. We then possessed nearly all of the public buildings and public works of the land, and they were objects of admiration. Strangers came from a distance to see them and enjoy them. The Fairmount Water Works, the old Bank of Pennsylvania, the old Bank of the United States (now the Girard Bank, both the works of Latrobe), the new Bank of the United States (now the Custom House), and the Exchange and the Mint of the United States, and the Naval Asylum (the works of Strickland), the old Philadelphia Bank, and such like, were scattered over our city, then small in its dimensions and population. Even in the earlier days we were not unmindful of what was due to good taste in the erection of our public structures, as well as in our beautiful private mansions that then stood surrounded with groves of trees adorning the town and country homes of our cultivated and wealthy colonial gentry and merchants. Let any one but step into Christ's Church, even as it is now changed by the renovating hand of modern improvement, and he will there see the remains of a harmony, simplicity, and fitness of adornment that indicates a high standard of just taste. And there is also the State House, in Chestnut Street. Enter the great hall that leads to the Hall of Independence and to the tower, on which is built the steeple, and there will be seen a passage of modest dignity, and a broad, well-constructed stairway, showing that even in those days, over one hundred and twenty years ago, when it was built, surrounded with the forest trees, and out of town—in those simple days our ancestors had provided, as we provide, for the future and for public purposes, with a liberal hand, regarding taste as well as utility. Let us not forget the Pennsylvania Hospital in Pine Street, with its spacious grounds and its lofty, stately main building, at this day an object of admiration for its size and its proportions, so suited for its purpose, and so simple in its quiet, harmonious beauty.

All this we still have; and, further, we have the Girard College, with other grand and elegant structures that are the work of our own days. I will not speak of them in detail; time will not permit me to describe the rows of new residences that adorn our streets, or the costly and stately churches that are scattered in every quarter of the town. You have the great Masonic Temple and three beautiful churches that cluster round this very spot. I can remember well when but two steeples rose above our town; now, as you gaze from the summits in the Park, the city lies before you with a number of lofty domes and sky-piercing spires. These are the work of private enterprise and bounty. We must not omit to remember the great gift the city has this day bestowed upon her people. To-day the Girard Avenue Bridge was delivered over to the authorities, and is now possessed by all of us. It is a work of wonderful merit, and is well worth the millions spent on it. It is an avenue worthy of any of the greatest cities of the world. It contributes to our convenience and prosperity, while it bears witness to our pride and liberality of feeling in all that concerns the common and public good. In our growth we live up to the example of our ancestors, and have resolved now that for our present necessities, and according to the abundance of our means, we will adorn our city as it was adorned of old, with a structure that will fully answer its end, and command the admiration of all men.

Such is my love for and faith in this city, that I feel possessed with a conviction, which might even be called a superstition, that it will again be, as it once was, the real metropolis of the nation. The capital and the public offices of the Union will never return ; the foreign trade may cluster at New York as it does in Liverpool ; but Philadelphia will be again, as she first was, the real centre of finance, of commerce, and wealth. She is at the head of the mechanic arts and of manufacturing, and she has ever led in refinement, in science, and in jurisprudence. The material supremacies which left her will return, and those graces and glories which she has ever had will never leave her. Here they made their home, where Penn, the greatest of all the founders of free commonwealths, demonstrated that liberty, the largest liberty, was compatible with obedience to law, and a colony, established to maintain the firmest of religious convictions by the strictest of sects, could protect all other beliefs.

This wisdom he transmitted to our people, and as a body they possess it to this hour as a spirit or living public soul, and it is that which has made us just what we are, and for which we are and have been conspicuous in all of our public history. In the Revolution, when we had most to lose, we were first in action, and faithful to the end, enduring all things, hoping all things, believing all things for the love of that Christian liberty which was a part of our blessed faith. In those sad days, here came, as to a common centre, all of the wise and brave who guided and led in that contest. Here the Continental Congress sat, here the Declaration of Independence was written, executed and proclaimed. After the Revolution, here George Washington presided over the deliberation of the Constitutional Convention ; and here, too, he administered to the end of his official life the Government he had helped to form for the country he had saved. How thickly the memories of these events, our great events of the past, press on me ! How the names of the wise and good and mighty rise up before me, and tempt me to enlarge upon the history of the grand things done, and of the men who did them. I mean those who belonged to us, who were Philadelphians, but whose fame is so large that men remember them only as belonging to mankind. We have had Penn and Franklin and Rittenhouse and Rush and Godfrey and Bartram, whose names posterity will not willingly let die. Penn and Franklin are names that never will be forgotten ; they will pass down through time linked with Solon and Lycurgus, Pythagoras and Archimedes and Socrates and Plato and Aristotle, the crowned monarchs of human thought. But I must here pause. I have well-nigh done all that was required of me. I must not wander off, tempted by these proud thoughts of our proud citizenship. I never approach a great building but with a sense of awe. Mechanically I lift my hat, as if I stood in the august presence of something grand and good. I can understand why men have imputed spiritual gifts to the masters of this the greatest of all arts.

For in it all science and all art unite to produce sublime and almost supernatural results. Solomon, the wisest of men, thus illustrated the highest reaches of his superhuman genius, and the greatest achievement of the chosen people was the vast temple built by that monarch and dedicated to the service of Jehovah. Go where you will on the face of the earth, you will there find these grand works of nations now dead and perished from the memory of men. Those who made them had immortal souls; but for this life they were mortal, and are no more remembered of men; and yet thus their history is recorded and remembered in monuments that were the works of their minds and hands— monuments that stand like great books written in the very rocks they are built upon. Where no such monuments are to be found the people had no mental or moral natures above the faculties of brutes. Wherever a nation had a conscience and a mind, there it recorded the evidence of its being in these the highest products of human thought, human knowledge, and human will.

It has been well said that architecture rests on two ideas—the natural, or the idea of order; the supernatural, or that of the infinite. In these various monuments of by-gone ages these thoughts are displayed according to the genius of the people.

"In Greek art order directs and guides the natural and rational idea. The strong column elegantly grouped, bearing at its ease a light pediment—the weak rests on the strong; this is logical and human. Gothic art is supernatural—superhuman—it is born of the belief of the miraculous and poetic. The geometry of beauty bursts brilliantly forth in the type of the Gothic architecture in the Cathedral of Cologne. To whom belonged the science of numbers, this divine mathematics? To no mortal man did it belong, but to the Church of God. Under the shadow of the Church in chapters and in monasteries—the secret was transmitted together with instructions in the mysteries of Christianity. The Church alone could accomplish these miracles of architecture. She could often summon a whole people to complete a monument. A hundred thousand men labored at once on that of Strasbourg, and such was their zeal that they did not suffer night to interrupt their work, but continued it by torchlight. Often, too, the Church would lavish centuries on the slow accomplishment of a perfect work."

The original and brilliant historian and thinker, whose words I have just repeated, citing them as the evidence of an observer, philosopher, and critic, conveys to us, in his clever sentences, those truths which illustrate and account for some of the most marvellous products of this mighty art. He reminds us that when pious zeal inspires, it passes beyond the mere love of order and fitness, and soars into the very empyrean of the miraculous and poetic. What a grand thing is it thus to perpetuate such sublimities of thought and feeling in monuments as everlasting as the hills, and as spiritual in their influence on the human soul! This is what we are doing. We are erecting a structure that will in ages to come speak for us as with "the tongues of men and angels." This work which we now do, as it were, in the morning hour of our being, will, probably, like the broken arch of London bridge fancied by Lord Macaulay, in some far off future day be all that remains to tell the story of our civilization, and to testify to the dignity and public spirit of our people.

What we thus give we must give with free spirit, not grudgingly, for as we are of great and good beginnings, and have been an earnest and noble race of men, so should we make this our monument tell the world and posterity how provident we are; how, scorning ugliness as we do vice, we resolve thus to speak to men as it were in words of marble, that in their order are logical and human, and in their form reach to the miraculous and poetic.

We have done and are doing a great, great work, and it will inspire our posterity to live up to our standard, as we are inspired to live by the standard of our ancestors. They loved their town with a gentle fondness that is testified by every act of their useful and remarkable public lives, and they transmitted to us, their sons, the same soft sense of affection. We, too, can say, as Franklin said when writing of his home— dear, dear Philadelphia. Do we not say it in enduring words with this day's work, and when we leave behind us this noble building to say it for us?

INSTRUMENTAL MUSIC.—National Melody, Potpourri— *Heinecke.*

BENEDICTION.—By R. W. Bro. Robert H. Pattison, D.D., Grand Chaplain.

INSTRUMENTAL MUSIC.—Liberty Polka—*Brill.*

OFFICE OF THE
COMMISSIONERS FOR THE ERECTION OF THE PUBLIC BUILDINGS.

PHILADELPHIA, July 7, 1874.

HON. BENJAMIN HARRIS BREWSTER,

My Dear Sir:

It affords me great pleasure, on behalf of the Commissioners, to request for publication a copy of the admirable Address delivered by you on the 4th inst., at the laying of the Corner Stone. The Commissioners feel under obligation to you for the research and labor expended in the preparation of the Address, which produced a marked impression on all who were so favored as to hear it, and cannot fail to go far towards satisfying the public mind of the necessity, expediency and wisdom of this great undertaking as it is now in process of accomplishment. The tone of thorough and heartfelt loyalty to your native city, and the full appreciation of its advantages and greatness which pervaded the whole Address, must have a most useful and salutary influence.

Trusting that an early and favorable response may be accorded to the above request,

I remain, very truly and respectfully yours,

SAMUEL C. PERKINS,
President of the Commissioners.

PHILADELPHIA, 13th July, 1874.

TO SAMUEL C. PERKINS, ESQ.,

President of the Commissioners
for the Erection of the Public Buildings.

Dear Sir:

I have been absent from town, or you should have had an earlier answer to your polite note of July 7th. I thank you and the Commissioners most cordially for the kind manner in which they make the request of me, and with this I send to you for publication the Address as asked for.

I am, with great respect, your friend,

BENJAMIN HARRIS BREWSTER.

.

SUMMARY

OF LEGISLATIVE AND MUNICIPAL ACTION RELATING
TO THE WORK, WITH A BRIEF HISTORY OF
EVENTS PERTAINING THERETO.

The earliest movements relating to the present undertaking consisted in the passage of an ordinance by the City Councils, approved December 31, 1868, providing for the erection of Municipal Buildings on Independence Square, and designating Commissioners to carry the same into effect.

The first meeting of the Commission was held in the Select Council Chamber, January 7, 1869.

Architectural designs were advertised for on the 5th of April, 1869, and on the 1st of September following, plans and drawings had been received from seventeen different architects.

At a meeting of the Commissioners, held September 27, 1869, the first premium was awarded to John McArthur, Jr., architect, of this city, and on the 27th of the following December, Mr. McArthur was appointed Architect of the work, and proposals for labor and materials were ordered to be advertised for.

Contracts were awarded on the 16th of January, 1870, and arrangements made for commencing the work.

A strong opposition to Independence Square, as the site for the Municipal Buildings, had existed in the public mind from the earliest movements in that direction, and as the

Commission proceeded with their preparations for carrying out the provisions of the ordinance under which they were acting, the opposition became daily more intensified, until it culminated in the passage of a law by the Legislature of the State, approved August 5, 1870, providing for the erection of the Public Buildings, either on Washington Square or on Penn Square, as the legally qualified voters of the City of Philadelphia might determine, at the general election to be held in October, 1870. The election resulted, out of a total of 84,450 votes, in a majority of above 18,800 in favor of the site on Penn Square, which finally disposed of the question. The passage of this law rendered the municipal ordinance of no effect, and relieved the Commissioners acting under it, of further duties.

The first meeting of the Commissioners, under the new law, was held on the 27th of August, 1870, at the Mayor's Office.

There were present Hon. Daniel M. Fox, Mayor of the City; Samuel W. Cattell, President of Select Council; Louis Wagner, President of Common Council; with all the Commissioners designated by name in the Act, except William Devine, deceased, and William L. Stokes, not known; and Messrs. Henry W. Gray and William S. Stokley were elected in their places. A temporary organization was effected by the election of Mayor Fox, as President, and Eugene G. Woodward, Secretary.

September 15, 1870, John McArthur, Jr., was elected Architect of the work.

October 4, 1870, a permanent organization was made, and John Rice was elected President, Charles R. Roberts, Secretary, and Charles H. T. Collis, Solicitor.

November 1, 1870, the Commissioners decided to have one building, and to locate it on the intersection of Broad and Market Streets, and on the third day of the same month proposals for labor and materials were advertised for.

The removal of the iron railings which inclosed the four squares on Broad and Market Streets, was commenced on the 27th of January, 1871, and this may properly be considered as the date of the actual beginning of the work.

At a meeting of the Commissioners, held June 19, 1871, a resolution was passed to the effect, "That any and all action heretofore had by the Board, designating the intersection of Market and Broad Streets, as the site for the Public Buildings, is hereby repealed, annulled, and made void;" and the Architect was directed to prepare plans for the buildings on the four squares, fronting on Market and Broad Streets.

The Architect submitted to the Board, August 7, 1871, designs for the four separate buildings, as directed, whereupon the same were adopted; and on the 16th of the same month the ground was formally broken by John Rice, Esq., then President of the Commission.

Impediments were from time to time interposed to the progress of the work, by application to the Courts on various grounds for injunctions, to which is to be attributed the delay which attended the early stages of the enterprise.

October 12, 1871, Francis De Haes Janvier was elected Secretary, in place of Mr. Roberts, resigned, and John Sunderland was elected Superintendent.

At a meeting of the Commissioners, held April 7, 1872, it was resolved to revert to the original idea of placing the buildings on the intersection of Market and Broad Streets. The architectural plans and drawings having been heretofore prepared for the work under the original instructions of the Commissioners, and the excavations answering in part for either location, the change from the four buildings to the intersection involved no delay. The first stone was laid on the 12th of August, 1872, and the work has since progressed without interruption and with great rapidity.

On the 17th of April, 1872, Mr. Rice resigned as President of the Commissioners, and Samuel C. Perkins was elected in his place.

The contract for the granite basement was awarded November 19, 1872, for $515,500; and work was commenced under the contract, March 24, 1873. The contract for the marble work of the superstructure was awarded on the 7th of October, 1873, for $5,300,000; and the first block set in the walls, July 3, 1874.

November 4, 1873, William C. McPherson was elected Superintendent, and entered upon his duties November 10th.

The appropriations by Councils for the prosecution of the work, have thus far been as follows:

For 1870, '71 and '72,	. $277,450 00
" 1873, .	. 770,959 88
" 1874,	. 1,457,450 00
	$2,505,859 88

Of this amount there had been collected by Special Tax:

In 1872, rate eight cents on the $100,	. $326,978 67
" 1873, " ten " " " .	469,972 68
" 1874 (to July 3d), rate ten cents on $100, .	347,701 88
Carried forward,	$1,144,653 23

Brought forward, $1,144,653 23

And there has been expended :

In 1872, .   . $155,933 64
" 1873, ... 435,137 92
" 1874 (to July 3d),   . 362,140 85
                                  —————— 953,212 41

Leaving cash balance, July 3, 1874, . $191,440 82

The Special Tax rate for 1874, was fixed upon an estimated assessed value of property subject to taxation of $548,243,535, which will produce, if collected in full, $548,244. The City Councils, however, have power to meet the appropriations made, out of the taxation for general purposes.

SINCE THE FIRST MEETING OF THE COMMISSIONERS,
THE FOLLOWING CHANGES HAVE TAKEN PLACE
IN THE MEMBERSHIP OF THE BODY.

1871. Jan'y 2. Henry Huhn, *ex officio* as President of Common Council, in place of Louis Wagner.
Oct. 19. Theodore Cuyler and Henry M. Phillips, resigned.
Nov. 15. William Massey and Mahlon H. Dickinson, elected in place of Messrs. Cuyler and Phillips.
1872. Jan'y 1. William S. Stokley, *ex officio* as Mayor, in place of Daniel M. Fox.
William E. Littleton, *ex officio* as President of Select Council, in place of Samuel W. Cattell.
Jan'y 2. John Price Wetherill and William Massey, resigned.
Jan'y 18. John L. Hill and R. J. C. Walker, elected in place of Messrs. Wetherill and Massey.
William S. Stokley resigned his individual membership. Henry W. Gray, resigned.
Samuel W. Cattell and Alexander M. Fox, elected in place of Messrs. Stokley (individually) and Gray.
Feb'y 13. Alexander M. Fox declined his election, and Hiram Miller elected in his place.
Feb'y 15. Louis Wagner, *ex officio* as President of Common Council, in place of Henry Huhn, who had resigned the office.

1872. April 17. William Brice and Thomas J. Barger, elected to fill up the number of Commissioners to thirteen.

May 14. R. J. C. Walker resigned.

May 28. John Rice resigned, and Richard Peltz elected.

July 12. Thomas F. Gaskill elected in place of Mr. Walker.

1873. Jan'y 6. A. Wilson Henszey, *ex officio* as President of Common Council, in place of Louis Wagner.

1874. Jan'y 5. Robert W. Downing, *ex officio* as President of Select Council, in place of William E. Littleton.

PLACES OF MEETING OF COMMISSIONERS.

The earlier meetings were held at the office of the Mayor. From October, 1870, the Commissioners met in one of the lower rooms of the new Court House on Independence Square until September, 1871, with the exception of a few meetings held at the Architect's office, to examine plans, &c. In September, 1871, rooms were rented for the use of the Commissioners in the second story of No. 1107 Chestnut Street, and occupied for a month, when the Commissioners removed to rooms in the second story of No. 1103 Chestnut Street. In November, 1872, the premises No. 1408 S. Penn Square, and opposite the site of the Buildings, were rented and are now occupied as the offices and place of meeting of the Commissioners.

4

No. 11.

Description of the Buildings.

THE EXTERIOR.

A tendency exists in the public mind to seek to classify every considerable architectural design, under the head of some "order" or "style;" but modern genius and taste deal so largely in original adaptations of classic, and other forms, that we often find no small difficulty in deciding under which, if any, of the heretofore established *orders* or *styles* many of the most important structures of the present day can properly be classed.

The architecture of the New Public Buildings is of this character. It is essentially modern in its leading features, and presents a rich example of what is known by the generic term of the "Renaissance," modified and adapted to the varied and extensive requirements of a great American municipality.

It is designed in the spirit of French art, while at the same time, its adaptation of that florid and tasteful manner of building, is free from servile imitation, either in ornamentation or in the ordonnance of its details.

This immense architectural pile is located on the intersection of Broad and Market Streets, in the City of Philadelphia. It covers, exclusive of the court-yard, an area of nearly 4½ acres, and consists of one building, surrounding an interior court-yard. The north and south fronts measure 470 feet, and the east and west fronts 486½ feet in their extreme length.

The four fronts are similar in design. In the centre of each, an entrance pavilion of 90 feet in width, rises to the height of 185 feet, having receding wings of 128 feet elevation. The fronts terminate at the four corners with towers or pavilions of 51 feet square, and 145 feet high.

The whole exterior is bold and effective in outline, and rich in detail, being elaborated with highly ornate columns, pilasters, pediments, cornices, enriched windows, and other appropriate adornments.

Archways of 18 feet in width by 36 feet in height, opening through each of the four central pavilions, constitute the four principal entrances, and at the same time afford passages for pedestrians up and down Broad and Market Streets, directly through the buildings.

The basement story is 18 feet in height, and stands entirely above the line of the pavement. Its exterior is of fine white granite, of massive proportions, forming a fitting base for the vast superstructure it supports.

The exterior of the building, above the basement, embraces a principal story of 36 feet, and an upper story of 31 feet, with an attic over the central pavilions of 30 feet, and over the corner pavilions of 12 feet, all of white marble, from the Lee Quarries, in Berkshire County, Massachasetts, wrought, in all its adornments, in forms of exquisite beauty, expressing American ideas, and developing American genius. The small rooms opening in the court-yard are each sub-divided in height into two stories.

In the centre of the group a court-yard of 200 feet square affords light and air to all the adjacent portions of the building. From the north side of this space rises a grand tower, which will gracefully adorn the Public Buildings, and at the same time will be a crowning feature of the city, from whatever point it may be approached, as Saint Peter's is of Rome, and Saint Paul's is of London. The foundations of this tower are laid on a bed of solid concrete, eight feet thick, at the depth of 20 feet below the surface of the ground; and its walls, which at the base are 22 feet in thickness, are built of dressed dimension stones, weighing from 2 to 5 tons each.

This tower, which is so deeply and so strongly founded, is 90 feet square at the base, falling off at each story, until it becomes, at the spring of the dome, an octagon of 50 feet in diameter. A statue of the founder of Pennsylvania, 20 feet in height, will crown the structure, and complete the extraordinary altitude of 450 feet, making it the highest tower in the world; while at the same time it possesses the elements of firmness and stability, in a higher degree than any known structure of a like character.

THE INTERIOR.

The entire structure will contain 520 rooms, giving ample, convenient, and stately provision for all the Departments of the City Government, classed under the heads of Legislative, Executive, and Judicial; besides which, a vast amount of surplus room remains for use in the classification and preservation of the archives of the city, for storage, and for increased accommodations, which will undoubtedly be required from time to time by the natural increase of the public business, and the accumulation of the public records.

Every room in the building will be well lighted, warmed, and ventilated, upon a thorough, effective and approved system, and every part of the structure will be absolutely fireproof.

The several stories will be approached by four large *elevators*, located at the intersections of the leading corridors, so as to facilitate the intercourse of citizens with the public offices, courts, and other branches of the government. In addition to these means of approach there will be large and convenient stairways in the four corner buildings, and a grand staircase in each of the centre pavilions on the north, south, and east fronts.

The following materials have been used in the foundations, and in the portions of the superstructure already commenced, to wit :—

    74,000 cubic feet of concrete foundations.
    636,400   "   " foundation stone.
    70,000   "   " dressed granite.
8,000,000 hard bricks.
    23,300 pressed bricks.
    36,972 white bricks.
      366 tons of wrought iron floor beams.
       6½ tons of wrought iron clamps.
      28 tons of cast iron lintles, askewbacks, drain pipes, iron bricks, &c.
    16,700 square feet of bond slate.

A large quantity of marble has been prepared for the superstructure.

The excavations for the cellars and the foundations required the removal of 141,500 cubic yards of earth.

The preparation of the ground for the excavations, involved the change of the gas pipes, and of the two water mains of 20 and 30 inches in diameter, from their course through the centre

of Broad Street, to a circuit around the site of the buildings.
The tracks of the West Philadelphia Passenger Railway were
changed from the centre of Market Street and laid around the
site; and the Freight Railroad owned by the City and which
ran through Market Street, was entirely removed after it had
ceased to be of use in the transportation of materials for the
buildings. These changes involved a heavy outlay, which was
charged to the Commissioners.

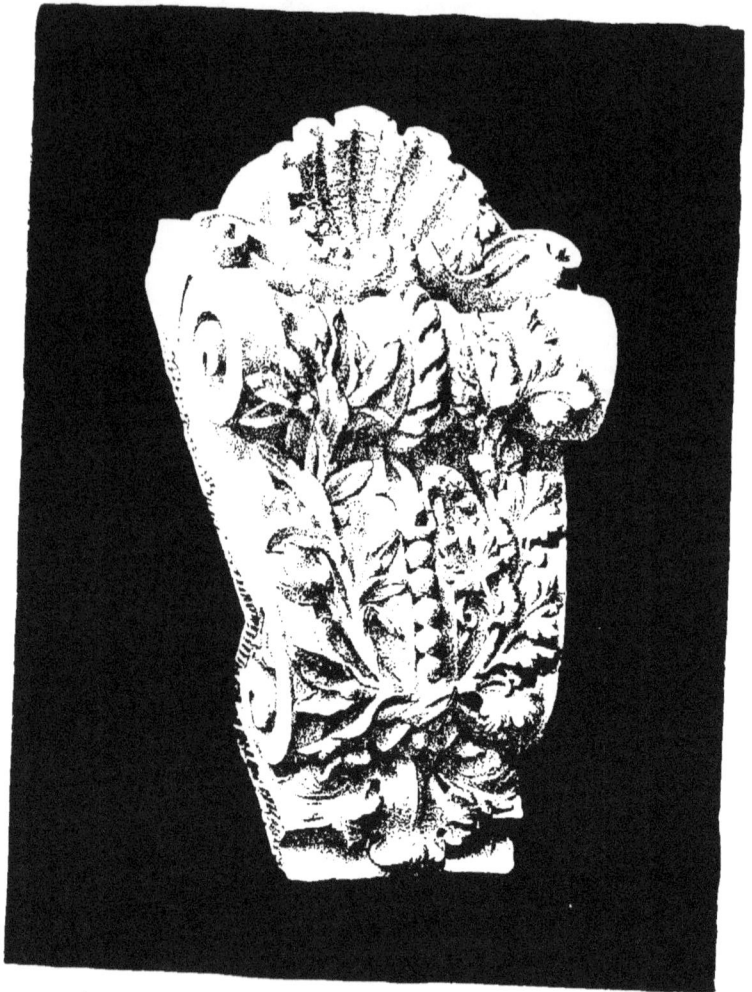

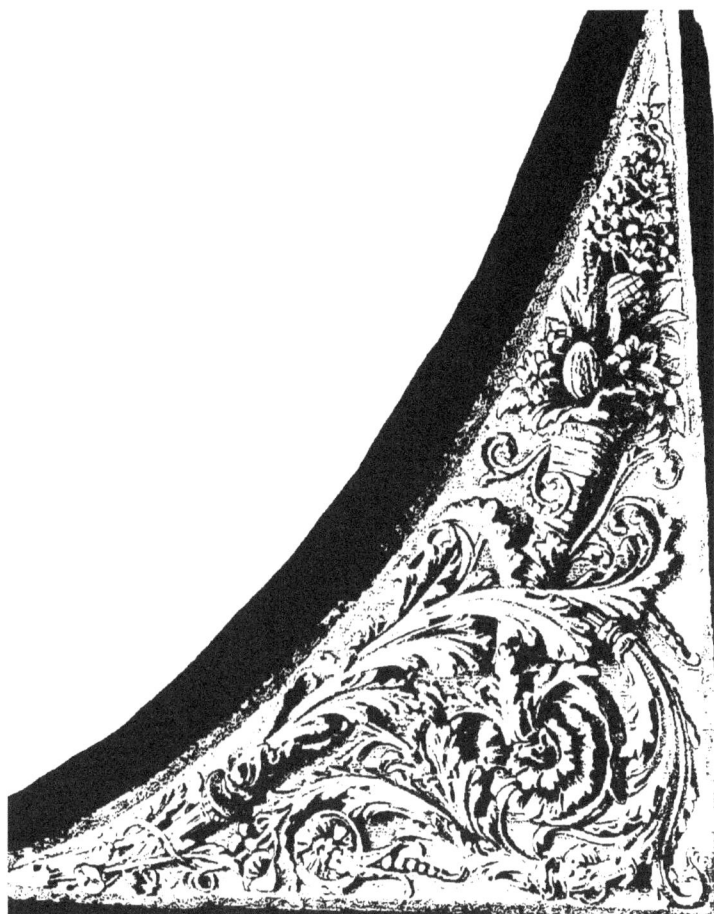

𝕯𝖊𝖙𝖆𝖎𝖑𝖊𝖉 𝕷𝖎𝖘𝖙 𝖔𝖋 𝕯𝖔𝖈𝖚𝖒𝖊𝖓𝖙𝖘, &𝖈.,

DEPOSITED IN THE CORNER STONE.

Constitution of the United States.
    "   " Pennsylvania.
Charter of the City of Philadelphia.
Elevation and Plans of the New Public Buildings.
Act of Assembly establishing the Board of Commissioners, with list of Commissioners and their Officers.
Programme of Ceremonies of Laying the Corner Stone.
Proceedings of the R. W. Grand Lodge of Free and Accepted Masons of Pennsylvania for 1873, with names of Grand Officers officiating in laying the Corner Stone.
List of Officers of the R. W. Grand Lodge of Free and Accepted Masons of Pennsylvania.
Ahiman Rezon.
Manning's Masonic Register for 1874.
Manual of Councils, 1874, containing Lists of the Members, and also of all Officers connected with the Government of the City and its several Departments and Public Institutions, and of the County Officers.
Annual Message of the Mayor, 1874.
First Annual Message of William S. Stokley, Mayor, and Reports of Departments for 1873.
Digest of Laws and Ordinances of the City of Philadelphia.

ANNUAL REPORTS OF THE SEVERAL DEPARTMENTS OF THE CITY GOVERNMENT.

55th Annual Report of the Board of Public Education.
39th   "   "   " Trustees Philadelphia Gas Works.
     "   "   " City Controller, 1874.
     "   "   " Department for Supplying the City with Water, for 1874.
     "   "   " Board of Health for the City and Port of Philadelphia, for 1874.
     "   "   " Directors of City Trusts, from 1870 to 1873.
     "   "   "   "   " 1874.

58

ANNUAL REPORTS OF VARIOUS PUBLIC INSTITUTIONS OF
PHILADELPHIA.

3d   Annual Report of the Presbyterian Hospital in Philadelphia.
1st and 2d   "   "   "   "   Home for Widows and Single
                                   Women, in the State of Pennsylvania.
13th   "   "   "   Board of Managers of the Women's Hospital
                            of Philadelphia.
20th   "   "   "   Board of Managers of the Howard Hospital
                            and Infirmary for Incurables.
46th   "   "   "   Board of Managers of the House of Refuge.
18th   "   "   "   "   "   "   Children's Hospi-
                            tal of Philadelphia.
9th   "   "   "   Jewish Hospital, with Ceremonies of laying
                            Corner Stone; also. an Engraving and
                            History of the Hospital.
6th   "   "   "   Board of Managers of the Philadelphia
                            Orthopœdic Hospital.
57th   "   "   "   State Asylum for the Relief of Persons De-
                            prived of the Use of Reason, 1874.
          "   "   "   German Society.
          "   "   "   "   Hospital of Philadelphia.
          "   "   "   Board of Directors of the Pennsylvania Insti-
                            tution for the Deaf and Dumb, for 1873.
          "   "   "   Philadelphia Dispensary for the Medical Re-
                            lief of the Poor, for 1873.
          "   "   "   Pennsylvania Hospital for the Insane, 1873.
          "   "   "   Board of Managers of the Hospital of the Pro-
                            testant Episcopal Church in Philadelphia.
          "   "   "   Board of Trustees of the Charity Hospital,
                            of Philadelphia.
          "   "   "   Christ Church Hospital, 1864, and Charter.
          "   "   "   Board of Managers of the Pennsylvania
                            Hospital, for 1874.

COPIES OF THE DAILY PAPERS OF PHILADELPHIA.

Press,   July 4, 1874.
North American and United States Gazette,   "   "
New Illustrated Age,   "   "
Public Ledger,   "   "
   "   Record,   "   "
Philadelphia Inquirer.   "   "

Philadelphia Democrat,	July 4, 1874.
" Freie Presse,	" "
" Abend Post,	July 3, "
Evening Bulletin,	" "
" Telegraph,	" "
" Chronicle,	" "
" Star,	" "
" Herald,	" "
" Programme,	July 4, "
The Day,	July 3, "
All Day City Item,	" "

COPIES OF THE LATEST NUMBERS OF WEEKLY PAPERS PUBLISHED IN PHILADELPHIA.

Sunday Mercury,	June 28, 1874.
" Dispatch,	" "
" Republic,	" "
" Morning Times,	" "
" School "	July 4, "
All Day City Item,	June 28, "
Keystone,	July 4, "
Saturday Evening Post,	" "
" Night,	" "
The Presbyterian,	" "
" Friend's Review,	" "
" Lutheran Observer,	" "
" Commonwealth,	" "
" Friend,	" "
Friends' Intelligencer,	" "
Trade Journal,	" "
Die Neue Welt,	July 5, "
Harness and Carriage Journal,	June 27, "
United States Railroad and Mining Register,	" "
Commercial List and Price Current,	" "
Christian Instructor and Western United Presbyterian,	" "
Chronicle and Advertiser,	" "
United States Journal,	June 26, "
Philadelphia Sonntags Blatt,	June 28, "
Reformed Church Messenger,	July 1, "
The Episcopalian,	" "
Vereinigte Staaten Zeitung,	" "
The Youth's Evangelist,	" "

The Germantown Telegraph,	July 1, 1874.
Shoe and Leather Reporter,	" "
The National Baptist,	" "
Insurance Reporter,	" "
The Lutheran,	" "
" Christian Recorder,	" "
Die Republicanische Flagge,	" "
Legal Gazette,	July 3, "
" Intelligencer,	" "
Journal of Applied Chemistry,	July, "
Temperance Blessing,	" "
Catholic Standard,	July 4, "
Illustrirte Zeitung, Leipzig,	September 27, 1873.

COPIES OF MONTHLY PUBLICATIONS ISSUED IN PHILADELPHIA.

Godey's Ladies Book,	July, 1874.
Lippincott's Magazine,	" "
Penn Monthly,	" "
The Amateur (Lee & Walker),	" "
Medical and Surgical Reporter,	June, 1874.
Catholic Record,	July, 1874.
Gardener's Monthly,	" "

Centennial	Almanac for 1874.
Public Ledger	" "
Lee and Walker's Musical	" "
Pocket Calendar	" "

Half Yearly Compendium Medical Science, January, 1874.

Election Laws, New Constitution, and State Officers.
Prospectus of the Philadelphia School of Design for Women.
Photograph, New Masonic Temple.
The First American Art Academy.
Exercises of the laying of the Corner Stone of the New Building for the Pennsylvania Academy of Fine Arts.
Address, Centennial Celebration of the Founding of the Pennsylvania Hospital, by Geo. W. Wood, M. D.
Brief Sketch of the Origin and History of the State Penitentiary for the Eastern District of Pennsylvania, by Richard Vaux.
Circular of the American District Telegraph Company.
Philadelphia and its Environs, by J. B. Lippincott & Co.
Officers of the Water Department for 1874.
Proof set of all Coins of the United States, for the year 1874.

MEDALS.

Presidential.—Ulysses S. Grant.

Washington.—Presidency Relinquished.

Army—Major-Genl. Jackson—Capture of New Orleans.

Navy—Capt. Bainbridge—Capture of the Java.

Sub-National—Penna. Volunteers—Action on Lake Erie.

Miscellaneous—" Let us have Peace."

        Emancipation Proclamation.

        Lincoln and Grant.

Contractors and Material Men.

REMOVING IRON RAILINGS.
Daniel McNichol.

REMOVING TREES.
Joseph Earnest.

EXCAVATIONS.
Wm. McLaughlin.

ERECTING FENCE.
Isaac N. Plotts.

SEWERAGE, AND REMOVING AND RE-PLACING WATER AND GAS PIPES.
Samuel Ogden,
John Campbell,
J. Wesley Miller,
Samuel J. Cresswell, Jr.,
E. Y. Shelmire,
S. Fulton & Co.,
Jesse W. Starr & Sons,
Clark Brothers,
Lucius Hart & Co.,
Water Department of Philadelphia,
Trustees of the Philadelphia Gas Works.

REMOVING AND RELAYING PASSENGER RAILWAY TRACKS.
Wharton & Bullock,
William Wharton, Jr.,
Samuel Mink.

REPAVING.
Daniel McNichol.

FOUNDATION STONE.
Conshohocken Stone Quarry Company.

LAYING FOUNDATION STONE.
Robert Armstrong.
Foreman, Samuel Scott.

SLATE BOND STONE.
D. Conway,
Wilson & Miller.

GRANITE WORK.
Philadelphia Granite and Blue Stone Company,
H. Barker & Bros.,
Comber, Sargent & Co.
John Comber,
Ezekiel C. Sargent,
Philip Dougherty,
John Müller,
John H. Killen.

MARBLE WORK.
William Struthers and Sons.
Wm. Struthers,
Jno. Struthers,
Wm. Struthers, Jr.

FREE STONE, &c.
Philip Dougherty,
Douglass Brothers.
Jos. M. Douglass,
Wm. S. Douglass.

BRICKS.
J. & A. Dingee,
H. K. Vandusen,
James Caven,
Excelsior Brick Company,
Lloyd & Russell,
Henry Huhn & Co.,
Benjamin Allen,
R. & W. McCay.

WHITE BRICKS.
Philip Neukumet.

BRICKLAYING.
J. B. Hancock & Co.

CEMENT.
French, Richards & Co.,
William N. Needles,
Paul A. Davis, Jr., & Co.

IRON BEAMS, &c.
Matsinger Brothers,
Steward & Stevens.

WROUGHT IRON WORK.
Charles S. Hughes.

CAST IRON WORK.
James V. Stileman.

HARDWARE.
Field & Hardie,
Wm. R. Elliott.

LUMBER.
Brown & Woelpper,
Esler & Brother,
Harbert, Russell & Co.,
Phelan & Bucknell,
Keeley, Brownback & Co.,
M. F. Stell & Co.
Geo. V. Keyser & Co.,
Daniel M. Williams & Co.

PAINTING IRON BEAMS, &c.
Charles Abel.

HOISTING MACHINES, RIGGING, &c.
Nelson Gavit,
John S. Lee & Co.,
Edwin H. Fitler & Co.,
J. N. Hoffman & Son,
John Baizley.

INCIDENTALS, STATIONERY AND PRINTING.
Fairbanks & Ewing,
James W. Queen & Co.,
Charles Williams,
King & Baird,
Wm. V. Murphy's Sons,
Henry B. Ashmead,
Thos. W. Price & Co.,
Allen, Lane & Scott,
Smith & Campion,
S. K. & S. D. Large,
Thomas W. Smith,
Isaac S. Williams & Co.,
Thackara, Buck & Co.,
D. Mershon's Sons,
James S. Earle & Sons.

PLASTER MODELS.
Alexander Calder,
Alexander Kemp.

PHOTOGRAPHS.
F. A. Wenderoth & Co.,
James Cremer.

MEASURERS.
John S. Thackeray,
Conrad B. Andress.

SURVEYOR.
D. Hudson Shedake.

Architect's Assistants.

R. W. PETERSON,   H. M. WILSON,
GEORGE T. PEARSON, THOMAS U. WALTER.

WASHINGTON B. POWELL,

JESSE L. FERGUSON.

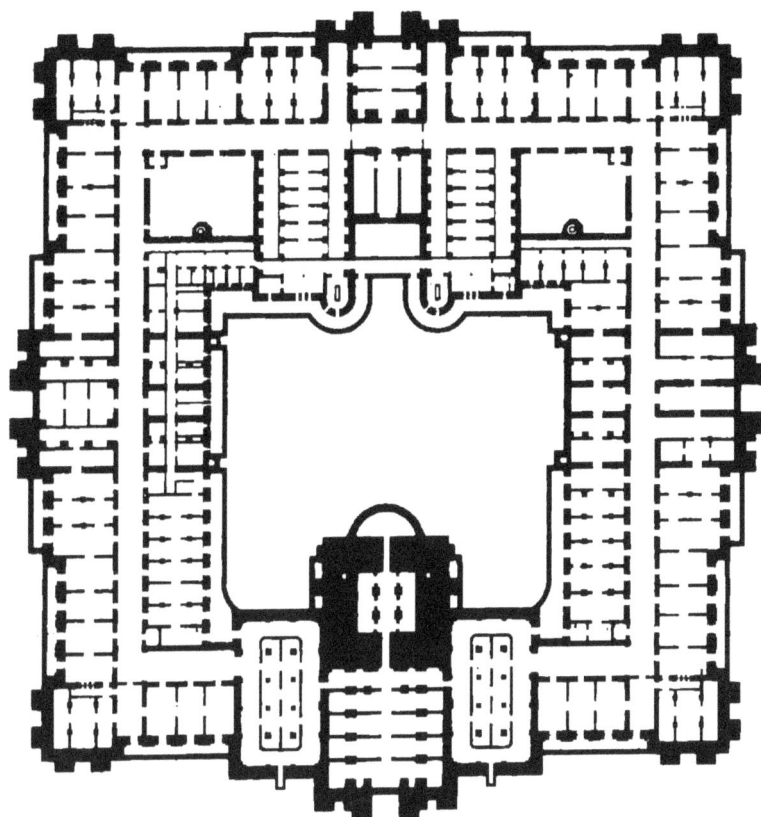

PLAN OF GROUND FLOOR OF NEW BUILDING

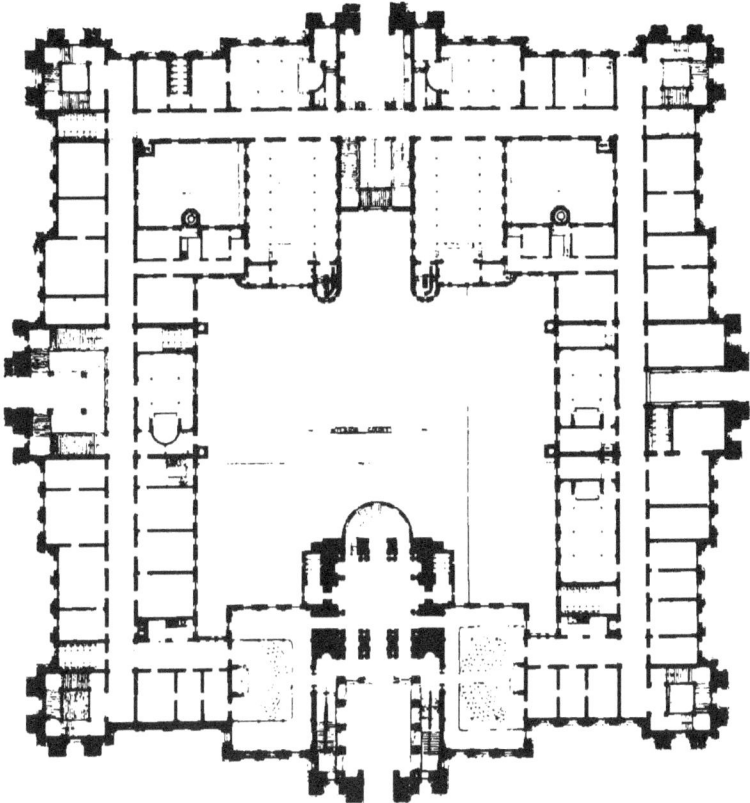

PLAN OF FIRST STORY INTERSECTION BUILDING

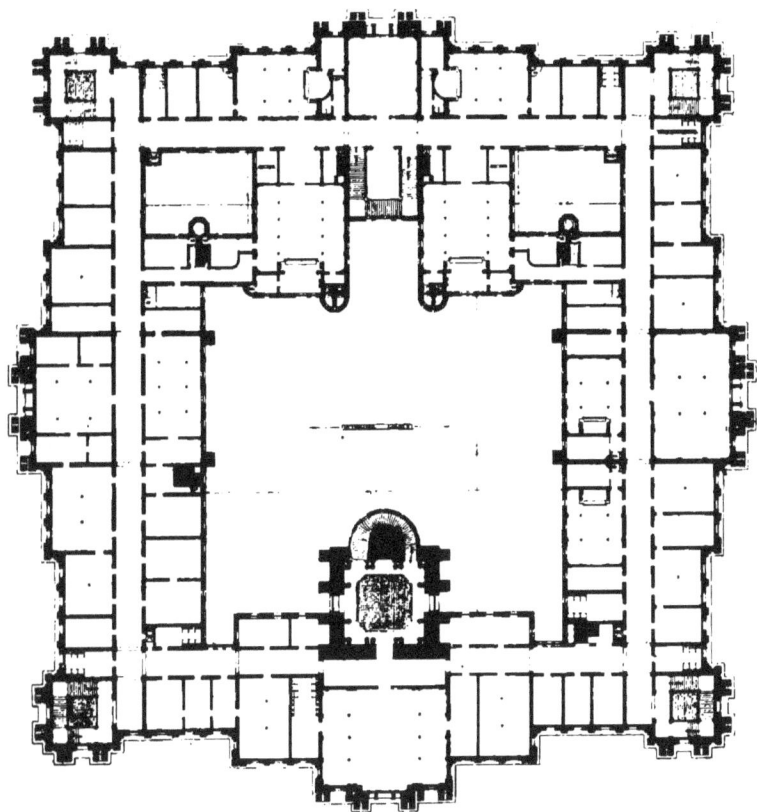

PLAN OF SECOND STORY • INTERSECTION BUILDING

www.ingramcontent.com/pod-product-compliance
Lightning Source LLC
Chambersburg PA
CBHW021411090426
42742CB00009B/1105